Bonjour, Piano!

ISBN 978-1-4950-8867-4

DURAND SALABERT ESCHIG
Editions Musicales

Visit Hal Leonard Online at
www.halleonard.com

CONTENTS

Editorial suggestions in the music appear in brackets.

COMPOSER BIOGRAPHIES

JEAN-MICHEL ARNAUD
(b. 1928)

Jean-Michel Arnaud was born in Paris. In his earliest piano training he was frustrated with a teacher who stifled creativity and improvisation. At age 12 he encountered more open-minded teachers at the Conservatoire. At 17 he began to teach in an unorthodox way, writing short pieces for his students and allowing them to choose the titles. This method was later crystallized in his piano method books, *Le Piano Ouvert, Le Piano Decouvert*, and others. Arnaud wrote lyrics for these pieces, and the other publications include recordings of himself and children singing along. He has taught piano in several schools in the Paris area, and has been invited to open "pilot" classes as alternatives to traditional music teaching. In addition to teaching, Arnaud has composed a string quartet, a quartet for string trio and flute, and a choral piece titled *La mu-si-que*.

FRANÇOIS COUPERIN
(1668–1733)

François was the son of the organist at Saint Gervais church in Paris. His father died when the boy was ten. Saint Gervais not only saved his father's position for the budding young musician and paid for his musical education, the church also paid for the housing and upkeep of François and his mother until he was old enough to assume the duties as full-time organist in 1688. In this period the royal court controlled all copyrights. Couperin obtained permission to publish his music. He was appointed organist of the King in 1693 and began teaching harpsichord to much of Parisian aristocracy. For the rest of his life he was regarded as one of the greatest teachers and keyboard players in France. Couperin published four books of harpsichord pieces, considered as landmarks of the French Baroque style. He was the author of a definitive treatise, *The Art of Harpsichord Playing*, addressing fingering, touch, ornamentation, and various other aspects of keyboard technique.

LOUIS-CLAUDE DAQUIN
(1694–1772)

A child prodigy, Daquin studied with his mother and at the age of six played the harpsichord for King Louis XIV. Two years later he was conducting his own compositions at the Sainte-Chapelle. At age twelve he became organist at a convent, the beginning of a series of high profile organist positions, including the Chapelle Royale, St. Paul's, Notre Dame, and Cordeliers. Daquin was considered one of the greatest keyboard players and improvisers of his time. He published much keyboard music, chamber music, and vocal music, much of which is lost.

CÉSAR FRANCK
(1822-1890)

César-Auguste-Jean-Guillaume-Hubert Franck was born in Liège, Belgium. His father, Nicolas-Joseph Franck, had hopes that the child would become a musical prodigy-composer like Liszt and make the family wealthy, so he entered him into Royal Conservatory of Liège for rigorous musical training. In 1835 Nicolas-Joseph moved with his sons to Paris. César studied composition at the Conservatoire, and he and his brother became quite active as performers. From 1847 to his death, Franck held a succession of organist posts, the most prestigious of which was titulaire at Sainte-Clotilde in Paris, home of one of the finest Cavaillé-Coll instruments. His masterful improvisations and compositions helped to inspire a wave of French symphonic organ style, and his *Trois Chorals* (1878) and other pieces have become essential organ repertoire. Most of Franck's mature compositions date from later in life, but he made significant contributions to several genres, including the Prelude, Choral and Fugue (1884) for piano, Violin Sonata in A Major (1886), Symphony in D minor (1888), and the oratorio *Les Béatitudes* (1879). His funeral was attended by such prominent composers as Saint-Säens, Fauré, Widor, and Chabrier.

OLIVIER HAURAY
(b. 1952)

Olivier Hauray was trained in organ and piano at the Caen Conservatory and with private teachers, and studied musicology at the Sorbonne. His career has been dedicated entirely to teaching piano; *Introduction to the piano by styles* volumes 1 and 2 are the result of his experiences as pedagogue confronted with the difficulties that student pianists have to solve. The books contain Hauray's original pedagogical pieces, emulating musical styles from Baroque to jazz, and proposing the technical solutions for their expressive purpose. Olivier Hauray continues to compose according to his musical encounters and his educational projects.

CHARLES KOECHLIN
(1867-1950)

Charles Koechlin was a prolific composer of diverse inspiration, ranging from impressionistic style to more chromatic, even quasi-serial techniques. He was born in Paris and attended the Paris Conservatoire, studying composition with Jules Massenet and later with Gabriel Fauré. His relationship with Fauré extended to writing the first Fauré biography and orchestrating Faure's suite from *Pelléas et Mélisande*. During his time as a freelance composer and teacher, Koechlin participated in several musical societies including the *Société musicale independent* and the International Society for Contemporary Music (ISCM). Koechlin made several trips to the United States with a special focus on the University of California, Berkeley. On his third trip in 1929, his symphonic poem *La Joie païenne* won the Hollywood Bowl Prize for Composition. Though rejected for a teaching position at the Conservatoire, he did join the faculty at the Schola Cantorum from 1935-1939.

PIERRE SANCAN
(1916-2008)

After early piano studies in Morocco and Toulouse, Sancan moved to Paris and studied with Yves Nat at the Conservatoire. He won several awards for his skills in composition and counterpoint, including the prestigious Prix de Rome in 1943 for his cantata *La Légende de Icare*. He achieved a teaching post at the Conservatoire in 1956, when Yves Nat retired. As a pianist, Sancan was highly regarded, though most of his public appearances were accompanying the cellist André Navarra. Sancan's compositions include an opera *Ondine* (1962), two ballets, two piano concertos, and advanced pieces for piano.

ERIK SATIE
(1866-1925)

One of the most eccentric personalities in all of music, Satie began piano studies in 1874, with a teacher who instilled a love of medieval music and chant. He entered the Paris Conservatoire in 1878, and was expelled two and a half years later for lack of talent. He was readmitted in 1885, but did not change the minds of his professors. After a detour in the Infantry – seen for a moment as a better career choice – Satie settled in the artistic Paris neighborhood of Montmartre in 1887. There he composed his first pieces: *Ogives*, for piano, written without barlines (a compositional choice found frequently in Satie's music) and the famous *Gymnopédies*. In 1890, while pianist and conductor at the cabaret Le Chat Noir, he met Claude Debussy and joined the spiritual movement Rose-Croix du Sâr Péladan (Rosicrucian Order), eventually becoming a choirmaster for the group. His involvement inspired the works *Sonneries de la Rose+Croix* and *Le Fils des Etoiles*. He had a brief and passionate relationship with the painter Suzanne Valadon in 1893. Brokenhearted after Suzanne left, he wrote *Vexations*, a theme to be played 840 times in a row – about twenty hours. In 1895 Satie abandoned his usual red robe and replaced it with seven identical mustard velvet suits, nicknaming himself "the Velvet Gentleman." In the next few years he moved to the suburb of Arcueil, and began taking composition lessons at the Schola Cantorum. He met Jean Cocteau, with whom he collaborated on the ballet *Parade* in 1916. Satie gradually met more artists of the French avant-garde, and presided over the birth of the group "Les Six." He died in 1925 of cirrhosis of the liver – probably due to his abundant consumption of absinthe. His friends visited his room in Arcueil – to which he had denied access throughout his life – and they discovered the state of poverty in which Satie had always lived.

HENRI SAUGUET
(1901- 1989)

Born Henri-Pierre Poupard, he used his mother's maiden name Sauguet when he began concertizing, to avoid embarrassing his father with activities in modern music. He studied the piano from an early age, and in 1916 became organist and choirmaster at Floirac near Bordeaux, taking organ lessons with Paul Combes. He studied composition first with Joseph Canteloube and later with Charles Koechlin. In his early career he met other notable composers such as Satie and Milhaud. Sauguet was a noted opera composer, with *La chartreuse de Parme* (1939) his largest-scale work in this vein. He composed several others over the course of his career, and for his first, *Le plumet du colonel* (1924), he even wrote the libretto. Sauguet also found success writing ballets, including *Les forains* (1945), about a traveling circus troupe. During the war, Sauguet used his status to help his many Jewish friends, while still producing an impressive amount of music, including his *Symphonie expiatoire* (1945), dedicated to the innocent victims of the war. Aside from composition, Sauguet was active as a critic for the French journals *L'Europe nouvelle, Le jour,* and *La bataille.* In 1976 he was elected to the Académie des Beaux-Arts in succession to Milhaud. He served as President of several organizations, among them the Union des Compositeurs, which he founded.

ALEXANDRE TANSMAN
(1897-1986)

Tansman was born in Łódź, Poland, but lived in France for most of his life. While in Poland he trained in music at the Łódź Conservatory and completed a doctorate in law at the University of Warsaw (1918). After moving to Paris in 1920, he met Stravinsky and Ravel, both of whom encouraged his work. Tansman found his way into the Ecole de Paris, a group of foreign musicians that included Bohuslav Martinů. Tansman enjoyed international success, with his orchestral music performed under such esteemed conductors as Koussevitzky, Toscanini, and Stokowski. During an American concert tour as pianist with Koussevitzky and the Boston Symphony in 1927, Tansman met George Gershwin. His concertizing also took him to Europe, Asia, Palestine and India, where he was a guest of Mahatma Gandhi in 1933. He gained French citizenship in 1938, but because of his Jewish heritage, he and his family were soon forced to flee France to the United States. Settled in Los Angeles, Tansman became acquainted with Schoenberg and composed a number of film scores. He returned to Paris in 1946. His honors included the Coolidge Medal (1941), election to the Académie Royale of Belgium (1977) and the Polish Medal of Cultural Merit (1983). He composed hundreds of pieces in total, exploring practically every musical genre, from symphonies to ballets to chamber music and works for solo guitar.

JEAN TRÉMER
(18??-1968)

Jean Trémer's name is attached to the *Hymn to Montmartre* (lyrics by Geo Duvic), the official hymn of the Republic of Montmartre (1934). He composed short piano pieces for children in two collections entitled *Les Petits Artistes (Little Artists),* published by Éditions Durand between 1932 and 1939. His career as a composer seems to have been interrupted by the war.

POINTS FOR PRACTICE AND TEACHING

Lullaby / *Berceuse*
from Three New Children's Pieces / *Trois nouvelles Enfantines*
Erik Satie

- Sometimes composers notate R.H. and L.H. on the same staff, and that is how this piece begins.
- A lullaby is a gentle piece by nature. Note that dynamics never move beyond p, and we are even asked to play **pp**.
- There is a variety of phrase lengths; notice the two-note phrases in m. 1-2 followed by a phrase over two bars in m. 3-4.
- Smoothness of phrase is important in capturing the character of this piece.
- Play with no pedal. The *legato* should come from the fingers.
- The R.H.'s gesture in m. 9 is played again into m. 10 at a dynamic of **pp**. Treat this as a slight echo.
- M. 17-22 are a repeat of m. 1-6.

In the Desert / *Dans le désert*
Jean-Michel Arnaud

- The L.H. pattern in m. 1-12 and m. 24-35 is known as "Alberti bass," a figure common in the Classical era. Keep the eighth notes even and steady.
- In m. 16-23, the R.H. picks up an eighth note figure outlining a chord, similar to the L.H. in the first section of the music. Again, strive for an even sound with no bumps.
- The repeated figures and slow harmonic changes also imitate the contemporary music style of minimalism.
- The composer has given specific pedal markings. The little peaks in the line under the bass staff represent places where you should change the sustain pedal.
- Clearing the pedal prevents harmonies from smudging together. Try playing m. 1-4 while holding the pedal down the whole time to hear the harmonies mix. This is what you should avoid.
- This piece is in ABA form. A: m. 1-15, B: m. 16-23 A: m. 24-38.
- Bring out the L.H. line in m. 16-23. The R.H. part, though higher on the keyboard, is an accompaniment.
- Read the text describing the desert scene. Try to think of the images while you play: the rocking of camels, the relentless heat, and more.

Street Singer / *Le chanteur des rues*
from Poetic Pieces, Book 1 / *Pièces Poetiques (prèmiere cahier)*
Alexandre Tansman

- The melody in the R.H. seems to be imitating an Italian song.
- Note the many dotted rhythms in the R.H. Make sure to play these rhythms correctly. A common mistake is to play the sixteenth notes early so that they sound more like triplets.
- Except for breaks in m. 6 and m. 14, the L.H. has the exact same *staccato* pattern from m. 1-24. Keep this pattern steady.
- From m. 25 to the end, the L.H. switches to *legato* phrases, while the R.H. has mostly *staccato* articulation.
- No sustaining pedal should be used.
- The sudden **ppp** dynamic in m. 40, as well as the mysterious harmony up until the end, might represent the street singer's sound fading as he walks into the distance.

Lullaby (The natural graces) / *Berceuse (Les graces naturelles)*
from Pieces for Harpischord / *Pièces de clavecin*
François Couperin

- The added articulations and dynamics are editorial suggestions, attempting to give a sense of style.
- Trills start on the note above.
- In m. 4-10, m. 12-14, and elsewhere, the L.H. part contains some unique phrasing (three slurred eighth notes followed by one *staccato*). Practice the L.H. alone.
- This piece should be played delicately, with a steady, even sound.

Waltz / *Valse*
Olivier Hauray

- Take time and don't rush, creating a beautiful tone for the R.H. melody.
- The L.H. in m. 1-8 has a very traditional waltz accompaniment (OOM-pah-pah). Notice how the bottom note holds through the entire measure.
- In m. 11-12, the L.H. thumb crosses under the third finger twice in a row. This particular cross may feel awkward at first, but it

will become comfortable if you keep your hand flexible and loose.

- The **Da capo al Fine** at the end means to start from the beginning and play through to the **Fine** at m. 8.

Waltz of the Marionettes / *Valse des marionettes*
from For Children, Volume 1 / *Pour les enfants, volume 1*
Alexandre Tansman

- In this piece, the R.H. plays melody starting on the downbeat and accompaniment on beats 2 and 3.
- Practice just the up-stemmed notes in the R.H. first to hear the basic melody. Then add the lower part.
- Work on finger independence to make the top melody prominent, while keeping the "oompahs" less loud.
- From m. 3 to m. 4, the R.H. has a finger substitution from 5 to 3 on the same A. Switch the fingers without letting go of the key.
- The material in m. 1-8 repeats in m. 17-24, but with a more active line in the L.H.
- The music evokes the sound of a circus or a music box.

Going for a Walk / *Promenade*
from For Children, Volume 2 / *Pour les enfants, volume 2*
Alexandre Tansman

- The R.H. has the melody while L.H. plays accompaniment.
- A consistent rhythmic pattern in this piece is a held note in the melody followed by three eighth notes.
- Make sure to hold the R.H. melody notes for their full value.
- Also hold the L.H. half notes for their full value, releasing on the downbeat of the next measure.
- In m. 9-16, keep the eighth notes steady between hands, like a well-functioning machine.
- Use no pedal.

Arithmetic Lesson / *Leçon d'arithmétique*
from For Children, Volume 2 / *Pour les enfants, volume 2*
Alexandre Tansman

- Tansman often emulated Baroque style in his music for children. Here he gives us a lilting dance in 6/8 time that most closely resembles a *gigue*, though at a much slower tempo.
- Perhaps the composer chose Baroque style for this piece to connect the logic of mathematics with the logic of counterpoint.
- The L.H. part consistently follows a quarter-eighth rhythm on each beat, with the only exceptions in m. 7-8 and m. 17, where it switches to eighth-quarter; and m. 10 and m. 18, where triplets appear.
- In keeping with Baroque techniques, Tansman includes many sequences in this piece. M. 3-9 form one long chain of sequences of various lengths, with an upward and then downward motion. This could represent working on a problem, solving it, and then moving on to the next problem.
- Notice the *crescendo* in m. 5-6, the arrival at *f* in m. 7, and then the *decrescendo* in m. 8-9. Work on shaping these dynamic changes.
- Relax the hands and practice slowly and separately.

The Marquis and Marquise / *Marquis et Marquise*
from Little Artists, Volume 2 / *Les Petits Artistes, volume 2*
Jean Trémer

- A *marquis* is a figure of nobility, someone who would have governed a certain region of land in olden times. The female version of the title is *marquise*.
- The music seems to represent a rhythmic courtly dance between the marquis and marquise. Imagine the two noble figures greeting each other.
- Hold the half notes in the lower R.H. part for their full duration.
- The L.H. requires careful coordination when moving down to new hand positions.
- The grace notes in m.12-13 should be played just before the beat. Do not over-accent them, since the dynamic is *p*.
- In m. 13-14, the L.H. second finger crosses over the thumb.
- No pedal should be used in this piece.

Music Box / *Boîte à musique*

from For Children, Volume 3 / *Pour les enfants, volume 3*

Alexandre Tansman

- Tansman imitates the delicate tinkling of a music box by setting the music very high on the keyboard. For easier reading, he has written the notes an octave lower with an *8va* marking throughout the piece.
- The dynamic *p* is important for capturing the music box sound.
- Keep a steady, mechanical tempo with no rubato.
- The L.H. encounters some difficult crosses of the second finger over the thumb in m. 7-10. Relaxing the hand is essential to achieving these movements.
- The lack of phrasing until the last two measures means that the notes do not have to be played *legato*.
- In m. 7-10, note that the L.H. fifth finger always returns to C. Practice returning to the C after each crossing maneuver.
- From m. 9 to the end, the music becomes more fragmented and full of pauses, until a *rallentando* in the last two measures. This represents the music box winding down.

Sophie's Waltz / *Valsez "Sophie"*

from For Small Hands / *Petite mains*

Pierre Sancan

- The R.H. has both melody notes and some accompaniment notes throughout the piece. Make sure the melody notes are always louder than the accompaniment.
- The accompaniment figures are frequently stated as two-note slurs.
- Note the opening mark from the composer: expressively. This should apply to both the opening melody and also the new melody at m. 37.
- The accompaniment trades back and forth between the two hands in an interlocking pattern. The hands should not be practiced separately.
- Note the imitation between the two hands in m. 16-20.
- In m. 52-55, the music slows down and fades. There's a sense of mystery about what will happen next. Take time and let the music hang in air before moving on to the next phrase.
- In m. 56, the L.H. picks up the opening melody of the piece, while the R.H. plays high accompaniment. Make the L.H. melody just as expressive as before.
- In m. 70-73, both hands suddenly move very high on the keyboard. Practice the fingering slowly and let your body rotate to the right for an easier reach.
- The marking *8va* means to play the notes under the dotted line one octave higher than written.

The Doll's Lament / *Les Plaintes d'une Poupée*

César Franck

- This sweet, slightly melancholy piece is in a loose ABA form. The second occurrence of A differs from the first in m. 53-62.
- Note the opening expression: *dolce*, or sweetly. Then at m. 21, *dolcissimo* - even more sweetly!
- The opening melody may seem simple, but the intrusion of some black keys later on adds complexity.
- The first half of the melody is made up of two four-bar phrases, and then the phrasing changes to every two bars.
- In section B, beginning at m. 29, the R.H. has a winding eighth note line. Then in m. 37-44, the L.H. picks up this line, repeating it almost identically.
- Notice how the L.H. accompaniment in m. 29-36 occurs on the downbeat, while R.H. accompaniment in m. 37-42 features most of the same notes, but played on beat 2.
- In m. 17-18 and m. 19-20, the R.H. switches from 2 to 3 and back to 2 on the F-sharp. This technique allows repeated notes to be played with more agility and less tension. In more advanced music, the pianist might be asked to alternate 1, 2, and 3 on a note repeated rapidly.
- Notice the thirty-second notes in m. 18 and 20. If this rhythm is difficult to understand, imagine a dotted-eighth followed by a sixteenth, except the sixteenth is divided into two equal notes.

Little Dream / *Petite rêverie*

from For Children, Volume 3 / *Pour les enfants, volume 3*

Alexandre Tansman

- The R.H. generally has two-note phrases. Slur the first note into the second, then lift to transition to new hand positions.
- Observe the frequent *crescendos* followed by *decrescendos* to make the music more expressive.
- Notice how the L.H.'s low notes in m. 1-3 move downward from E to B, outlining a harmonic progression.
- The L.H. has some difficult reaches in m. 4, 8, 9-12, and elsewhere. The jumps from a low E fifth to G-sharp in m. 11-12 may be exceptionally difficult. Practice a smooth, fluid motion that allows your hand to move with freedom.
- If this piece tells the story of a dream, what is the dream about? The general character is mysterious.

The Happy House / *La Maison Heureuse*

Ten Easy Little Pieces / *Dix Petites Pièces Faciles*

Charles Koechlin

- The R.H. and L.H. generally have the same rhythm, with some extra melody notes in the R.H. The melody is always the top note. These factors give the piece the sound of a chorale or hymn.
- The meditative, quiet mood evokes a contented family living in peace.
- In m. 9-10, the R.H. plays two notes in the bass staff. Follow the r.h. and l.h. markings.
- Look at the long phrase in m. 7-10. Try to shape this as you build to the highest note in m. 9.
- On beat 2 of m. 4, the R.H. has a dotted eighth-sixteenth rhythm in the top voice and two eighths in the bottom voice. Practice this slowly.
- Sustain pedal should be used in this piece.

Sleeping Doll / *Dormez "Doll"*

From For Small Hands / *Petite mains*

Pierre Sancan

- Sancan has written many *tenutos* in the L.H. chords. Sink into these chords, hearing them support the R.H. melody. Despite the *tenuto* markings, make sure to release during the quarter rests.
- In m. 9-17, the two hands imitate each other rhythmically, following each other up the keyboard. Keep the two lines independent and equally strong, like a dialogue between two hands with the L.H. leading.
- It is especially important to emphasize the L.H. *tenutos* when the notes clash against the melody, as in m. 14. The dissonances may sound odd, but if you play them confidently and beautifully they will sound more convincing.
- Follow the *decrescendo* in m. 24 to provide a magical color change for the chord in m. 25. Notice that the notes of the chord are restated in an arpeggio over m. 25-27, while the pedal is held. Sancan wants us to savor this harmony.
- This arpeggio spans a wide range, requiring the L.H. to cross over the right in m. 27 before the R.H. plays the last note.
- Beginning with the unexpected C natural in m. 28, Sancan restates the opening melody of the piece in the R.H., with some unpredictable shifts in the L.H. accompaniment. Practice the L.H. in m. 28-39 alone to hear the long descending sequence.

The Doll / *La Poupée*

from For Children, Volume 1 / *Pour les enfants, volume 1*

Alexandre Tansman

- The first three notes in the R.H. form a motive that repeats fourteen times over the course of the piece. Though the fingers are closer together than usual, practice the motive slowly to prevent rushing.
- Hold all of the dotted quarter notes in the R.H. for their full value.
- Keep a steady, rhythmic energy throughout the piece.
- Note that in m. 3 and m. 6, the R.H. plays the third finger on A, then fourth finger on A on the way back down.
- Practice the L.H. slowly and separately.
- Based on the character of this piece, what do you imagine this doll looks like?

The Cuckoo / *Le coucou*
from Harpsichord Pieces, Book 3 / *Pièces de clavecin, troisième livre*
Louis-Claude Daquin

- The cuckoo is a bird whose distinctive call is often referenced in music, literature, or in the famous cuckoo clocks.
- Daquin has written the cuckoo call first in the L.H. in m. 1-4, then in m. 15-18, and then in the R.H. in m. 23-31.
- The sequence in m. 5-9 contains some tricky fingering in the R.H. A shorter version appears in m. 19-22. Practice these sections very slowly until the frequent hand position changes become more comfortable.
- The ornaments in this Baroque piece have been written out as sixteenth notes to prevent confusion. See m. 4, 10, 13, 18, 22, and 32.
- Make sure to keep the staccato notes short to capture the true cuckoo sound.

Go to Sleep, Little Brother / *Fais dodo, Colin, petit frère*
from Little Artists, Volume 2 / *Les Petits Artistes, volume 2*
Jean Trémer

- The title is an English translation of the famous French children's song "Fais dodo Colas, mon p'tit frère." The recognizable melody begins at m. 5.
- This piece presents thicker textures than those up to this point.
- The L.H. has some tricky crosses in m. 1-4 and again at m. 17-18. These involve the second finger crossing over the thumb, then the thumb over the second finger, then sometimes back to the second finger again.
- If it is too hard to reach the L.H.'s highest notes in the previously mentioned bars while still holding the low note with the fifth finger, use the sustain pedal.
- Notice how in m. 9-12, the L.H. imitates the R.H. a beat later. Emphasize the imitation by playing all the accents.

The Spinning Top / *La Toupie*
from For Children, Volume 2 / *Pour les enfants, volume 2*
Alexandre Tansman

- Don't be intimidated by the constant stream of sixteenth notes. Notice that the L.H. plays the same four-note pattern in m. 1-4 and 7-8, and the R.H. part in m. 1 is repeated exactly in m. 3 and an octave higher in m. 7 and 9.
- The repeated pattern in the L.H. evokes a top as it spins round and round.
- Practice both hands separately except for the interlocking patterns in m. 5-6.
- This is a classic example of a piece that sounds harder than it is to play. Once you master the sixteenth notes in both hands, you will achieve a very sophisticated sound.
- The repeated E's in the R.H. in m. 6 are marked with a specific fingering pattern. Classical piano technique almost always asks for alternating fingers on repeated notes. Feel the key rebound as you play each new finger.
- You'll see the same repeated-note fingering in the last measure, with the fourth finger employed on beat 3. Slow practice is essential.

– Brendan Fox
editor

Lullaby

from *Three New Children's Pieces*

Erik Satie

Gently, slowly [♩. = c. 50]

In the Desert

Jean-Michel Arnaud

Under a blazing sun,

a caravan advances
one hears the moaning of camels

and the light song of a flute.

Suddenly,

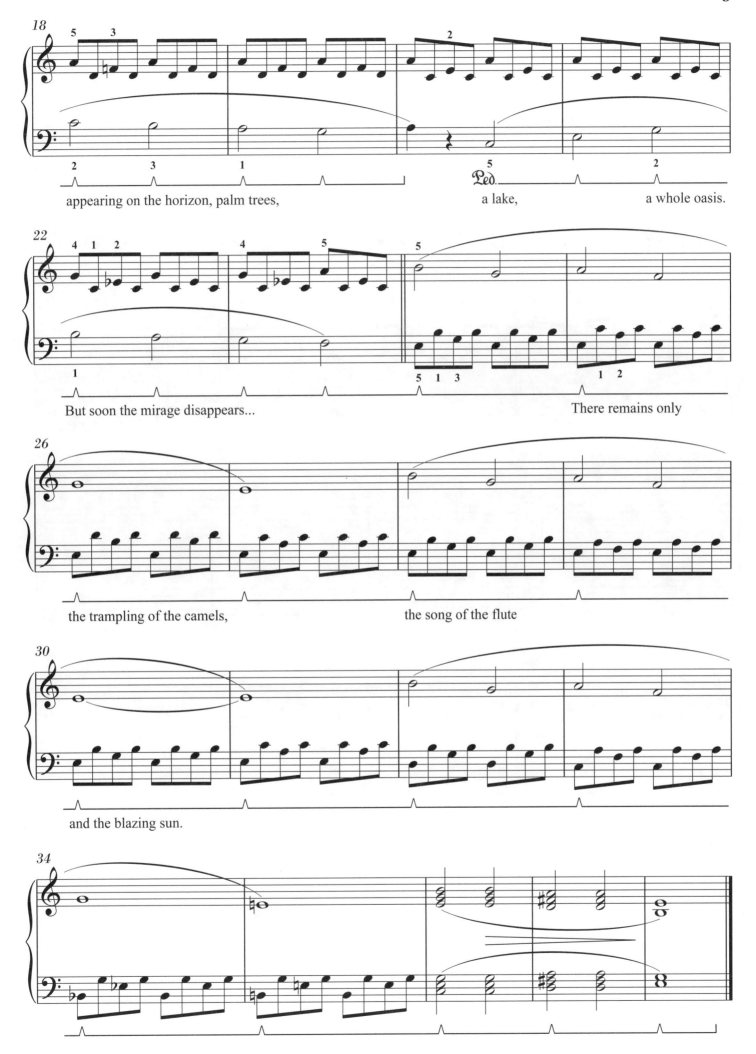

appearing on the horizon, palm trees,   a lake,   a whole oasis.

But soon the mirage disappears...   There remains only

the trampling of the camels,   the song of the flute

and the blazing sun.

Street Singer

from *Poetic Pieces*, Book 1

Henri Sauguet

Lullaby
(The natural graces)
from *Pieces for Harpsichord*

François Couperin

Tempo, articulations and dynamics are editorial additions. Trills begin on the note above.

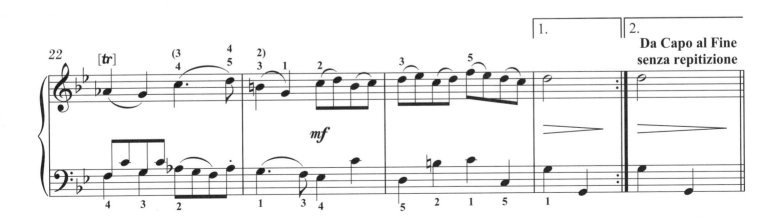

Waltz

Olivier Hauray

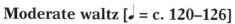

Saving room for a footnote.

Waltz of the Marionettes
from *For Children*, Volume 1

Alexandre Tansman

Going for a Walk

from *For Children*, Volume 2

Alexandre Tansman

Arithmetic Lesson

from *For Children*, Volume 2

Alexandre Tansman

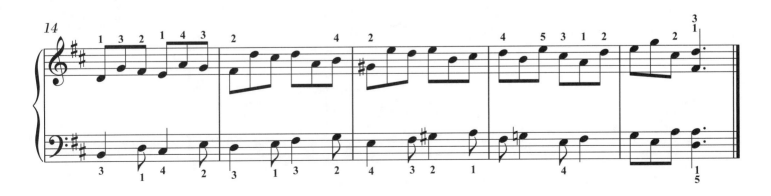

The Marquis and Marquise

from *Little Artists*, Volume 2

Jean Trémer

Music Box
from *For Children*, Volume 3

Alexandre Tansman

Moderately [♩ = c. 80–86]

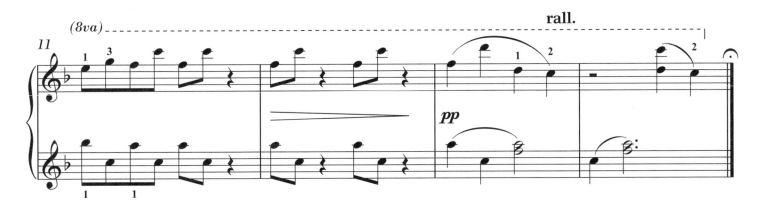

Sophie's Waltz
from *For Small Hands*

Pierre Sancan

The Doll's Lament

César Franck

Little Dream

from *For Children*, Volume 3

Alexandre Tansman

The Happy House

from *Ten Easy Little Pieces*

Charles Koechlin

*Tous droits réservés
pour tous pays*

Sleeping Doll

from *For Small Hands*

Pierre Sancan

This page has been left blank to avoid unnecessary page turns.

The Doll

from *For Children*, Volume 1

Alexandre Tansman

The Cuckoo
from *Harpsichord Pieces*, Book 3

Louis-Claude Daquin

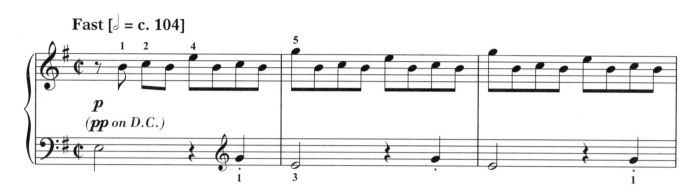

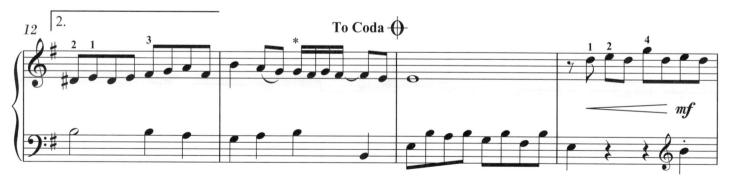

Articulations and dynamics are editorial additions. Ornamentation has been notated for this edition in places marked with *. The original notation was in 2/4, changed in this edition to 2/2.

D.C. al Coda
(with repeat)

CODA

Go to Sleep, Little Brother

from *Little Artists*, Volume 2

Jean Trémer

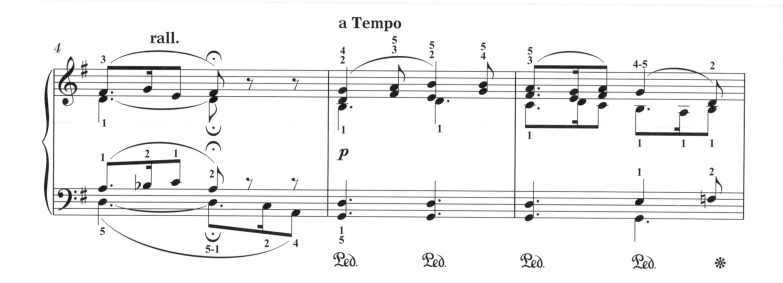

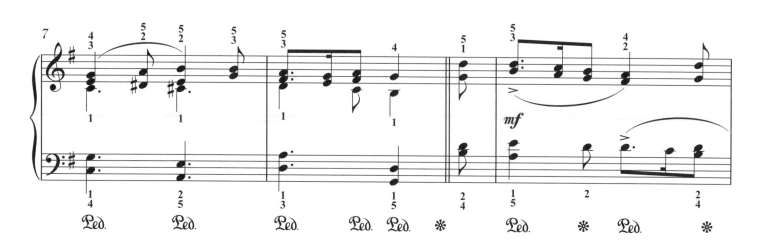

The Spinning Top

from *For Children*, Volume 2

Alexandre Tansman